Niké

AND OTHER POEMS

ROBERT BAGG

Azul Editions
2006

"Body Blows" is a revision of the title poem in *Body Blows: Poems New and Selected* (Massachusetts, 1988). Many thanks to *North Dakota Quarterly* for publishing "Niké: For Richard Wilbur," "The Closest Thing," "Clyde Torrey," "Dream Wife," "Spirit Spouse," "The Poet Who Couldn't Write a Poem to His Wife," "An Ancient Quarrel," and "Horsegod," and to the *Just Good Company* website for posting "Chimera."

Imaginative, ingenious and (sometimes) drastic editorial suggestions from Donald Junkins, James Scully, and Mary Bagg helped many of these poems shed some of their clumsiness, obscurity, prolixity, and, best of all, their inhibitions.

This limited first edition
is published by
Azul Editions

ISBN: 1-885214-21-9

Printed in the United States of America
10 9 8 7 6 5 4 3 2

Azul Editions
www.azuleditions.com

Other Books by Robert Bagg

Translations:

The Oedipus Plays of Sophocles (with Mary Bagg)
Hippolytos by Euripides
The Bakkhai by Euripides

Poetry:

Body Blows: Poems New and Selected
The Scrawny Sonnets and Other Narratives
Madonna of the Cello: Poems

Contents

For Mary, who insisted

The Names of Perfumes

Abruptly slams the bathroom door.
Water explodes from both taps, then a sound
I do not recognize at first impacts
like rock crunching as it hits porcelain,
seven, eight shatterings. Then silence
tightens the skin of the door's huge bass drum.
I pound it, she unlocks; a fragrant barrage
lavender, lily, pine, grass, musk

invades me. She stands naked, right foot braving
water savagely hot, jagged with glass,
the labels tearing in the swirl, *Chamade,*
the roll of drums before surrender, *Arpège,*
Arc de triomphe, Fleurs du mal, Vol de nuit,
Prends-moi, Huitième voilette, Force majeur.
Sliding gently down the tub's curvature,
glass shards cutting her buttocks, she turns

to look. I pull her upward, thighs and back
blood-pocked. She spits out *Tarc, Majette,*
Malheur, Têtehuit, Cège, Corf, Phiore,
Maudeur, T'aime, t'aime, t'aime!
Glazed eyes, a scream that crazes them, woman
in pain, all things I once squeezed into sense
are nouns disintegrating, consonants
lacerating, vowels melting in my brain.

Rules

We're working through our last June day
together. I must be home by dark.
In baseball weather, we plant roses,
winging our feelings back and forth,
a game of burnout going nowhere,
each word aimed where the last stung.
"Why do I want my wife more
than I want you?"
                    "It's in the rules,
Champ. Tie goes to the wife."

"Sooner Murder

an infant in its cradle than nurse an unacted desire."
— Blake, "The Marriage of Heaven and Hell"

At the Chanticler in Gourdon

Four dine while a child wakes, a fire roars.
The wife intently sips her Lynch-Bages,
likes it so much she kisses her host's cheek;
then offers hers. While guests avert their eyes
she lifts her child to soothe him with her milk;
her breast gives gently; the child feeds, then sleeps.

Her husband drives them up to Courmettes peak
from which the *hommes oiseaux* are taking off —
he thinks of riding his own thermal down
on Dacron wings, sprinting toward sky, trusting
the air to carry him where he won't feel
those hungry mouths and sweetly offered breasts.

Spells

1.

You begin with one fingernail: sharp
on the underside of my wrist.
Your breath probes deeper, a warm wind
teasing the noses of my drugged mates —
you call each reticence by name:
Honorbound, Spiritpeace, Homesafe,
They wake up sniffing, licking your fingers,
searching your lap, your hair, your mouth.
What you whisper makes their teeth
turn playful, grazing your skin, tamed.
You stroke the beast from their bodies,
each one now a free man, rubbing his eyes —
my old crew, my bodyguard! — come with me
this far, this bloody far, once
willing to die, willing to kill, for me.
Are they loyal to me still? Or to you?

2.

I try to warn you of danger
by showing you a poem: wherein
a kiss wears slowly, cruelly off.
A woman has been changed
into a poem before your eyes.
Your arms tingle, you feel sick.
You cannot sleep. So you fight back:
It must not happen to you.
But look, you are already *here.*
We live by casting spells, we die

curing ourselves of them.
This poem will hold you a while.
I will hold you a while.

Lutte sans Cesse

1. He Reads Austen

She flees the dancing in a neighbor's coach,
reliving the night's repartee with her mamá.
A month gone by, she learns her magic words
were "blissful whirling" and her clinching touch
the hand she left in his, four seconds longer
than should reward a man who's danced with her
but once. Just to be married is enough.
She asks no more of either life or him.
He asks just this: Marry our daughters well.

2. She Reads Tolstoy

She sees him riding with his regiment,
his mare so stubborn it takes both his calves
crushing her sides with every surge to hold
her body to the star-crossed, wheeling ranks.
Though they have danced, and sung Italian songs,
and loved, it was his fierceness in her sleep
bathed her in sweat until it woke the prince —
her pleasure ebbing, her hands clenched, her red mouth
screaming for love to crush her one last time.

3. Dénouements

I told you novels would not help us much.
Our Nicoles and our Heathcliffs go their ways.
Their stories pluck them from the hotel curb
in limos we can't stop or chase or find.
We're left with constitutions strong enough
to suffer through a dozen dénouements.

You were so deeply loved, you now can die.
But we are living in the house we chose!
I want your life. Your body wakes from love,

4. Unbathed Bodies

the prince's caviar lingering on your breath,
your unbathed body holding on to mine.
You wake from someone else's passion in our bed.
And so do I. But we are waking up.
The ends of novels kill their marriages.
A poem where nothing's final is our friend.
Today, nothing will happen. You will cook,
I'll greet our neighbors on a famous beach.
We'll swim, we'll kiss farewell. Love is *lutte sans cesse.*

1839: The First Man

1.

The first man
photographed

drinks water

from a pump
in a Paris square

vein thin   ink black
an etching
in acid

by Daumier   he

incarnates thirst   keeps

quenching

mouth glued
to rising water

one boot
on the iron rung
stove
        pipe
                hat

cocked forward

unaware
        silvery
chemicals

devour on a glass plate

his very life

2.

Still thirsty

at the *Café Bonheur*

he pours
        himself
Perrier

whose bubbles

swarming off the bottom

gradually

unseethe

a glass   within which

nothing

happens

Body Blows

For George Amabile, Rome: Winter 1962-63

You hang tough on a Roman street corner
shaking your thick dark head to clear it
from a punch to your mind no one saw land,
whose force you shrug — as a dog
throws water from drenched fur.

A quarrel with your wife before dawn
sends you barreling north on via Cassia,
the night air cold, your anger hard.
You steer by moonlight down the centerline.
So does the man you hit head on —
shot from his Vespa, his head
a rock, crunching the windshield, his body
bouncing over the roof and gone,
his Vespa pummeling your bumper
as you slew sideways churning gravel.

You grope for a dying body, but
find an indignant throbbing man
whose neck from a lifetime booming
soccer balls has stopped this great one.
You help him to a cinder bank,
you feel that Miura neck
pulse under blood-clotted hair.

No one believes this man survived.
Carabinieri comb the bushes and rubble
for the real dead — you've hired Rocco
to save your rich American neck.

But Rocco is persuasive: It's his Vespa,
his own neck's gorgeous muscle,
your million Lire in his mind.

When the police subside, you and he
link arms, throw grappa back,
enter each other's lives.
You buy him a new Vespa;
he sells you mantis-thin
Etruscan bronze his brother bathes
in urine so it ages fast,
gaunt green gods you give to friends
as brilliantly authentic fakes.

Before you vanish into Vecchia Roma,
you send pregnant Prudence to Little Rock.
Weeks later in a bar you tell me
what happened: "I was lifting Pru
like Pluto lifts Persephone
before ravishing her in Hell —
she felt my fingers like the god's
denting her thigh — at that
she freaked and yelled,
'Get out!' I did."

"Don't say a word" (you pummel me,
you hit me with your palms
weaving them like a boxer).

"Put dents in your own poems, Man,
let 'em take life's best shot."

Later, in the Piazza Navona,
empty at midnight, you halt
blocking my way with these words:

"My head took a worse shot once —
from a kiss that touched down like a moth
on my cheek while I crashed from beer —
it was a kiss from Him, the great
kind man you and I loved and loved,
but never with our bodies, as he wished.
That kiss lit up the abyss.
I'm still falling."

You fall while you speak, calmly and backward.
Your head pounds ancient paving stone,
its bone-hard blow delivered loud
to churches and palazzos
and to my gut. You stand up,
shake that black skull one more time,
go off to douse it in Bernini's
brimming tub of reveling giants
still after centuries raucous, splashing
shine over their stony beards
and bellies, gaunt knees and huge balls.
Nightwater greets our plunging faces —
spouting and drinking and shaking
the chill off among those other battered,
already frozen beasts and gods.

Niké: For Richard Wilbur

At the American Academy in Rome, 1958-1996

We writers were assigned the old potter's shed,
its kiln and dislocated wheel nearby,
built on the slope below the Aurelian
Wall that swells up from seething Roman earth
like a Pacific roller cresting overhead
— a perfect wave to catch, if you can ride
that buried power surging underfoot.

Out its south windows stretched the backyard farm —
ten walled-in acres of working campagna.
Free-ranging hens skittered about, women
picked blue-green artichokes into aprons,
a goat's vibrato rasped and rasped and raaaasped.

Cool morning winds bending the tulip beds
brimmed over us, setting our hands to work.

When nothing much was happening on pages
littering our worktable, we would feed
the woodstove wretched balled-up early drafts
better off smoke than fodder for critics.

Time to quit writing when the noon cannon
boomed over Rome from Garibaldi's statue.
Afternoons we trooped down to the Tiber;
our scholar-guides ticked off on either hand
snake-throttled bell towers of the late Baroque,
or probed the Palatine with a miner's cap
to spotlight, in a second-century school,
graffiti mocking Gaius for his faith.

At night, Fellini and Frascati binges.
Fired by such trips we hiked back to write late,
through artichokes whitening in the moonlight.

Every writer left something odd behind.
Letters from convicts to Ralph Ellison,
Louis Simpson's unpublished dissertation
on James Hogg, the Ettrick Shepherd,
a photograph of Tony Hecht's young wife
stunning herself on what looked like Capri.

Pinned to the back wall for contemplation
were single words, writ large in lithe italic
script. Some I recognized as nouns vital
to Richard Wilbur's Roman fountain poems:

a Greek word, *Arêté*; a Latin one,
reticulum; then *laundry* and *angel*.

That wall of opportunity beckoned:
Don't hide your most audacious words — flaunt them!
Rescue them from Roget. Get them ready
to rise to your occasions. Poems are made
not just from serendipitous *mots justes*
but from words groomed until their big chance comes.

One word of Wilbur's never got the call.
At least I never found it in his poems.
Niké: a goddess once, but now a shoe —
an airborne winner riding roughshod.

Wilbur left it, a tuft of flowers spared
for those who work this meadow after him.

What I heard, though, wasn't morning gladness,
but Frost's raw harsh voice — *you work t'gether,
Buddy, whether you work t'gether or apaart.*

Though tempted I let Wilbur's *Niké* be.

Whatever Roman fact he made a poem
soars in its place, even his railway station's
Jordanesque swoosh of roofline hangs there still —
beyond the faked-out past, beyond my reach.

Poets compete for fame. Is this our worst
infirmity? Or just our union card?

*I'll scavenge Rome for transient artifacts
too fleeting for Wilbur or never etched
by Piranesi; I'll go easy on fountains
in favor of totaled Vespas and time bombs.*

What seemed a small refusal now seems huge.
I should have put those Nikes on and run.

Thirty-eight years later I just do it.
The farm is gone; American grass, green as
a fairway, soothes the Fellows dealing frisbies.
Our boarded studio stores beat-up chairs.

Niké is still pinned to the burlap wall
in Wilbur's hand, breathing inside her ink
cocoon, impatiently growing wings.

The Closest Thing
Ginsberg in Paris, Corso in Rome

> Poetry
> pardon me for having helped you understand
> you are not made of words alone.
> — Roque Dalton, "Ars Poetica 1974"

Without any exaggeration, I'm still, if not the best, at least
the closest thing to what a poet should be. The more I read
these Cambridge poets the more I'm convinced of this.
These New England poets, apocalyptic crocodillions,
the whole horde of them. They do not realize that poems
are nothing without the poet. Why are Shelley, Chatterton,
Byron, Rimbaud, to name but a few, so beautiful? I'll tell
you why, they and their works are one and the same,
the poet and his poems are a whole.
  — Gregory Corso, Letter to Hans, ca. May–June 1956

Heretical doctrine once, Gregory, more like gospel to me now.

To that young Jersey Crocadoodle you sang at in Paris,
    though,
chanting "Marriage" to Sally and me off the Champs-
    Elysées,
poets' lives could be thrilling but not works of art;
poems came to life solely as words on a page,
rising to no occasion beyond their own artifice.

Amherst taught me that, which I had to unteach myself.

Still, just who, what, is Corso's wholly fused poet and poem?
To this day I'm not sure. But when I heard Beat poets live,
their chattering bodies scribbled all over my skin

psychic tattoos of invisible ink, to be developed over time.

I was writing my name in the Transients' Register
at the Paris American Express — Ginsberg's name
lit up the page above mine! In the column where
he declared his Final Destination, *Heaven*,
to my chagrin I'd written, "Cap d'Antibes."

I sent a note, hoping to meet him. He replied!
"Be there demain, à six heures, au Café Bonaparte."
He saunters to Gay Paree's epicenter, shouting "BAGG,"
then spends the next hour telling me sonnets are poison,
pentameter's dead! Drop, he advised, out of Amherst,
the Academic School of Uptight Verse, don't become
a Merrillian poodle or worse, a Wilburnian loon.
Go back to Homer's pulsing hexameters,
listen to Whitman — only lines with that kind of reach
can take in any and all sensations flowing by, the deluge
of people, of bed-fellows, butcher-boys, bathers, spinster
       voyeurs;
feel him breathing America, inhaling her exhaling her
on the smoke of his own breath. That's poetry!
the smoke of your own warm breath realized
in the chill of the air swirling around it.

I didn't buy his scary advice, but do so now —
       at least for today!
Dear Ginsberg, no question you spread yourself thin. Yet . . .
even Merrill declared, you spread yourself over
       the entire field
of American verse like a good healthy layer of manure.

"Come see us in Rome," I urged Corso the day he read
"Marriage," his version of J. Alfred Prufrock —
strangled by a tie on a third degree sofa,

should I say this, should I do that — a Prufrock
ungelded, unbuttoned, word mad!
"We'll pay our respects to Ovid Catullus Keats
Shelley Byron Fellini," I said, never dreaming
he'd actually spring for such a pilgrimage,
but by Ginsberg, he did — hunting me down in Rome
deep in the stacks of the American Academy
on my knees with a catalogue drawer in my lap.

We hiked up to my rickety study, plastered like a hornets' nest
to the old Aurelian Wall. There Corso made his mission clear:
"Bagg, I'm gonna be Shelley, so you can be Thomas
    Jefferson Hogg.
We'll get kicked out of Yale together for mooning Bloom!
You'll be my best buddy, you'll write my life, I *love* your two Gs.
And I promise not to live long, a little less than Shelley,
a little more than Keats, just long enough to slaughter Prose."

For nearly a week, we hung out. On via Veneto one evening
he asked every tart on the street if she was the mom
who'd left him to a bad dad, worse fosters, an orphanage,
street crime and a prison with a library, unknown
till Ginsberg's wandering eye for lost souls spied
Greg dealing down poems at a bistro in the Village.
Soon Corso was camped out at Harvard, alighting in Frisco,
made a fourth for Kerouac, Ginsberg, and Burroughs.
Their wildcatting books hit gushers of thick black gold.

I learned from him, from Corso, that making a poem of your life
is hot sweaty work, especially in sweltering Rome.
One morning at dawn in the Foro Romano he hurled himself,
full length, like a visionary torn from a sprawling
    Russian novel,
at the Oxford-shod feet of Lily Ross Taylor, Bryn Mawr's
Professor of All Things Roman, salaaming his gratitude

for learning so much about bricks, baths, Caesars, and those
Vestals he surprised in the gardens of Brattle Street,
    Cambridge.

Lily tip-toed, barely breathing, past his dusty adulation.

That very midnight we drove in my Volkswagon Beetle
over the jaw-jarring stones of the Appian Way,
me steering, Corso on the back bumper, one hand
on the luggage rack, whipping those 45 horses
past the crucified slaves, flaming fifty-gallon drums,
orange faces of mini-skirted whores warming their butts.
I wish I could leave you there, Gregory, a Delphic
    Charioteer
losing his grip on those runaway Horses of the Sun.

Except . . . there's one more scene to this story,
    the grand finale,
perhaps meant to show you in action taking down Prose,
the Poetry Eating Dragon, or perhaps you're Percy Bysshe
Corso, outraging your way to a noble expulsion.

I did not witness what happened, but pieced it
together, like Thucydides, from eyewitness accounts.
They'd invited Corso to lunch, the Academy Fellows.
He thought their scholarly in-jokes offensive,
their passion for trivia unbearable, brutish, insensitive
to the demons driving the very artists they studied,
unfeeling his need for "a young mad beautiful pope."
To exorcise their emptiness, he offered up himself
as everything they were not, climbing aboard the forty-
foot-long refectory table, toeing soup bowls aside,
strutting himself up like the Catullus Yeats imagined,
denouncing the lot for never using "masturbate"
in any of their writings, for never having slept, like him,

in the Colosseum's character-building chill and dirt.

A burly Virgilian caught and lifted him aloft,
set him off in the Billiard Room to cool down.
Within minutes Corso was back, pounded open the doors,
hailed the Classics Prof as his personal Caesar,
knelt in prayer to be granted new life, miming thumbs up
or thumbs down, to the crowd judging him from above.

He had thrown himself on their mercy, thrown down one final
roll of the poet's dice, turning those Fellows to Romans
holding this gladiator's life in their bloodless, bloodthirsty hands.

Caught in his script, the scholars voted him up,
but when he vaulted back on stage, yelling "Truth Pyre!"
they hustled him out to a cab that roared him away,
back to Paris and the acrid fame he'd earned from BOMB,
his poem cheering on the human nuclear deathwish.

Forty-four years later, his wish fulfilled, he came back to Rome
as ashes, to be buried in the Protestant Cemetery,
his prostrate headstone nestled near Shelley's charred heart
bravely but gingerly seized from Percy's burning corpse
by Edward Trelawney, the pirate manqué, on Viareggio's beach.

Ave atque, Gregory, from we who believe but cannot commit
Roque Dalton's "Ars Poetica," teaching us, as you did,
that poetry isn't made from words alone, but inflicts
itself on every soul within soulshot: an Improvised
          Enlightening
Device, whose urgency we deny to our grief.

Horsegod

Outskirts of Rome, 1996

You could disappear from the earth you walk —
leave with no warning this Italian farm
whose family rakes red olives off the trees —
go the way of all flesh but in free-fall,
the world as bottomless beneath your feet
as Satan's, falling nine days down your mind.

Earthly creatures disappear — just like that.
Suburban paisanos report their draft
horse missing near Hadrian's Villa
the afternoon we toured some outbuildings —
once barns, or barracks, for imperial troops.

The horse was foraging around a steep hole —
in one quick flash this staring oculis
blinked him underground, imprisoning him
inside the ancient cryptoporticus
that runs for miles below Hadrian's vista.

He returns every morning for his hay, thrown
down the same ugly hole through which he crash-
landed in stagnant water and farm debris.
It was in fact garbage of centuries
that softened to the stone floor his kicking bulk.

How will they ever get him out, we scholars
wonder, staring at those pungent depths.

Impossible to free our minds of him —
unharnessed animal life so rampant
it will do anything to leave its dark.

We will do anything to leave *our* dark.

I park in the steep vale below the farm,
walk up the road, avoid the barking cages,
the lit doorways, the probing searchlights.

Fifty yards past that treacherous eyehole
I find the brush-clogged entrance and edge down,
a pouch of sweet molasses feed in hand,
a lead and halter, but I mostly bring
memories of horses frightened in the night.

Water is wicking up my trouser legs.
I make too much noise sloshing through mud.
After a hundred yards, I can smell him,
then hear his tranquil breathing become charged.
He sniffs and snorts at me, his rough tongue
sandpapers my wrist, and then finds the oats.

I slide the leather halter up and over
his head and ears and click the latch. He's mine.
Andiamo, I tug, *Vai, vai!* Back to
our lives! But he won't budge. He won't be led.
I grab his clotted but deep-rooted mane
and drive my knee against his side, pull my length
across his back, like a live pallet, then work
my legs around so I'm astride. Now he'll go —
his body hardens with still-clenching muscle.
I edge my right heel back along his side,
tuck my head to his neck, feel his ears poke
out straight, and out of rotting earth we churn

reanimated halves of the one beast
both of us want mightily to be: the Horsegod!

We pound through reeking sludge and angry brush
that claws our faces, snags our thrusting legs,
we are joy pulsing through a line of verse!
A black hole chases us every word
of our way out, and will wait for us — there
at the far end of all our sentences,

here in the restless farmyard where we rest.

I feel our mouth tear sweet grass from the earth,
our shuddering legs go suddenly still.

I slide off, free the halter, watch him canter
off toward Hadrian's stables still in use.

Clyde Torrey

For Donald Junkins

Thoreau he wasn't — nor did life in his shack
resemble *Walden*; though like Henry, Clyde
was a sociable loner. Years back, this foundered
mail-boat captain, whiskey-eyed, had misread
the rip churning between Swans and the Sisters —
an error punished by the Red Point ledge.
Within an hour the island's fire brigade
had tackle hitched and winching from spruce trunks,
ratcheting Clyde, stern-first, toward quiet water.
That one-way crossing was his last command.

Don and I met him farming for a living
on two acres of seaside campground, plowing
behind Sandy, his clump-hoofed Belgian.
When someone asked for an autograph,
he wrote, "Clyde Torrey, Farmer, waiting
for my Maker." In cold weather he hunkered
in a junked sedan with a space heater
on the back seat, the Celtics or the Sox surging
and fading downeast as Clyde piloted
a dark road, bumping under tireless, cinderblocked
wheels. Mornings, he stretched his feet back down
to earth, soggy with bourbon and kerosene fumes.

Two nights one winter, Don and Clyde kept vigil,
a shotgun ready for a deer sniffing apples
by moonlight — a dream of venison cleaned,
bled, hung, eaten for weeks. It never showed.

When neighbors brought leftovers to his door,
Clyde let them ripen and make do: day-old cod
for chowder, then bait. One summer, he plowed
his field with a warped dinghy rudder. Huge
garbage bags stuffed with clattering soft drink
cans, lugged off by ferry to Bass Harbor,
came back in Clyde's overalls as *Jim Beam*.

Etta Morrison baked him a cake
every year on his birthday — angelfood
iced with meringue, or chocolate-hearted
devil's-food — thinking Clyde would wish
and blow their blazing candles to oblivion,
but each year's cake sat on the topmost shelf
where it stiffened — just so many birthdays
gathering dust. "What Clyde Makes of Birthdays"
became the text for a sermon Don preached.
The ravens and seraphs he freed from Clyde's cakes,
now airborne, hovered over the pews
at the Atlantic Baptist Church, patiently
searching our faces for somewhere to roost.

The morning after Clyde burned down his house
with a knocked over candle — the ashes too searing
at dawn for us commiserators to rake through —
his nephew's backhoe rumbled through the fog,
ground to a halt, and lowered to Clyde's field
a chicken coop held gently in its jaws.

An Ancient Quarrel

**within a Profession Shaken
by Cultural and Political Agitation**

How would the world be luckier, Yeats' poem asked,
if the proud clan at Coole Park went under,
bankrupted by tenants threatening trouble
unless sold back the land stolen from them?

Yeats had named in his poem what Coole gave back
to Ireland: "the arts that govern men . . .
And gradual time's last gift, a written speech
wrought of high laughter, loveliness, and ease."

The tenants won, the great house was knocked down.
But Yeats' own chanted speech survives nearby.
Hear it resonate from loudspeakers hung
in that square stone Tower fused with his life:

"image of solitary wisdom won by toil."
Thoor Ballylee cost him thirty-five pounds;
its value-added did not come from ease.
In our own time I put another question

to those who, in the next century, will
teach Yeats and all the other Great White Males
who offend — genius profiting mightily
from privileges of gender and of class,

whose poetry is punished resolutely
lest its pleasures disorient the young.
When you teach Yeats — I should say *if* you do —
what's vulnerable will stare you in the face:

from his escapist "Innisfree," his smug boast
that he recruited gunmen with a play,
his loony world of masks and moons and gyres,
his unrequited love of country folk,

his praise of fascists European and homegrown,
but most of all his fierce artistic pride
that consciously insults all lesser minds —
declaring men of vision rightly claim

the largest share of what their vision sees.
"I thirst for accusation," he admitted.
There is no doubt his cup runneth over.
What does this flood of accusation do

for you accusers? Something unforseen.
When you say Yeats is arrogant and crazed
by turns — that he championed violence,
magic, the unjust torque of wealth and birth,

that he exaggerated what his friends achieved,
wrote poems alloyed with so much folly
they shrivel seething in your mind's sulfuric —
guard against excess passion in your voice.

You might be stirring forces hard to quell —
that thrill exploding in your abdomen
when a trapped quarry turns his fear on you.
You go in flailing hand to hand, frenzied

because your own survival's now at risk.
His barbarous thrusting voice impales you
deep in the place from which your war-cry soars.
Now it's the pure joy of battle driving

your righteous censure and *his* bitter song —
you are Cuchulain hacking at the waves,
Yeats' music an invulnerable tide
that keeps on singing from each mortal wound.

Final Exam

Phi Beta Kappa poem
Nu Chapter of Massachusetts, 26 May 1990

"My heart aches, and a drowsy numbness pains
my sense, as though of hemlock I had drunk . . ."

"That is no country for old men,
the young in one another's arms . . ."

"I grow old . . . I grow old,
I shall wear the bottoms of my trousers rolled . . .
I shall wear white flannel trousers and walk upon the beach."

Essay Question

"Dear Students: what do these lines stolen
from famous poems all have in common?
Relate their power
first to the body of the poem, then
to some experience in *your* life, which the poem
illuminates."
                    I lift a giant hourglass from my desk,
baton-twirl it upsidedown:
"Don't be mesmerized by the flowing sand.
Work your page. You *must* finish this exam."

My students wear work clothes on exam day, no bright frocks,
but sweat pants, dance leggings, combat fatigues.
They write on desks gouged by graffiti from yesteryear:
Shakespeare lives! This professor lives in outer space.
A few ballpoints push off
downstream, others

cross out whole pages, rocks
ripping holes as thoughts crest and submerge.
One man's pen pauses for minutes on the edge
of a vast plain with blue rivulets.

I share their settings out —
later today, coffee mug in one hand,
I'll climb aboard each student's raft,
my own pen poling
soberly in the margins.

Not grading just yet, but
imagining as the sand flows,
I read their busy faces.

"Professor, I could use two or three
beakers full of the warm south
myself right now,
especially since I haven't read
Keats' "Nightingale" since last March . . ."

"Keats' drowsiness colors the whole ode,
which is life's bad news always coming true . . ."

"Old Prufrock is a classic wimp,
but he's gutsy,
he makes me feel great
picturing *him* eating his heart out on her sofa
while she plays out her mind games . . ."

The last grains land on the small dune
in my hourglass. I strip the stragglers
of their blue books, pack them up,
skimming though a couple
as I walk up the stairs.

One steals my own question and carries me
outside into the Amherst sunlight:
"What do all these gloomy-gorgeous lines have in common?
They fight what time does to us —
men lose their nerve, women their looks,
desire dies, people die — it's a sad
harsh scene out there. But somehow poets
turn misery into ecstasy. What should
we nonpoets say when our friends die of AIDS,
or in a car crash, or when we know we're losing it?
No poetry wand
touches the sore places. It's not
that poetry's useless —
we just use it in weird ways. Example:

Michael and I were walking Nauset beach
last Sunday, studying for the exam. I
kissed him, then headed toward the dunes
thinking he'd follow and catch me.
Mike rolled his trousers up
and walked that beach
half way to Provincetown. See —
you have us thinking like Mister Eliot.

Except Prufrock means different things to us.
Mike meant to say he's nobody's Prufrock — *his* beach
leads on and on to blanketfuls of sunbathers
he'd just as soon check out as play my game.

Mike and I can talk Yeats together too.
We are his "young in one another's arms" —
we dying generations — at our songs.
Not to be disrespectful, sir, to you or Yeats,
but why do you believe that just because
we're caught by sensual music, we

neglect monuments of unaging intellect?

When Mike came back from Nauset beach
he read me poems. Dozens. Wallace Stevens'
"She sang beyond the genius of the sea"
he said over and over.

I heard all genius singing
in Mike's hesitant, passionate,
Massachusetts voice. Was Mike himself
a male monument, or what? Then he stopped
speaking poems and said, "Marry me."
What I said then is — to use favorite words
of yours — beyond the scope of this course.

I have a question now for you, Professor.
Why does it take so much music
squeezed into little lines in books
to make Mike know I am worth loving and we're
both going to die? Why did I weep at Mike's
two ordinary words — Marry me! — and not once
at those grand marvelous lines that dared him
to speak at last in his own voice?"

I write: "Nice Work — A minus.
Catherine, there *are* no ordinary words.
Poets know this. That's what they teach.
But there are page tears and life tears.
When life tears are about to fall, page tears
evaporate. Yeats also wrote:
'Life is a preparation for something
that never happens.' Maude Gonne
did not say to him, 'Marry me.'"

The Poet Who Couldn't
Write a Poem to His Wife

Sure, fiery poems can be sparked, like pearls,
when minor irritants surround themselves
with tiny glittering worlds of sheen.
Think Herrick, suddenly drenched as Julia's dress
brushes, like a mermaid's wake, his packed codpiece;
remember Catullus, irked by Lesbia
letting her sparrow peck her lap with his beak —
both allumeuses flamboyant forever!

Expect no such poem from the likes of him,
whose woman comes on as a long slow wave
rising from their lives' imploding undertow,
a woman who wears only seawater,
her love a conch held roaring to his ear,
receding only to build slowly again.

A Cry

in a dream is noiseless
but it can still be very loud,
loud enough to wake its dreamer up,
as Mary's frozen-mouthed cry just did me,
though she's beside me, sound asleep —
or was, because my typing this
a room away inspires her
to come inspect the noiseless words
darkening the sheet you now read.

Spirit Spouse

*Spirit Spouses are small carved wooden figures used by
certain African tribes to comfort living spouses whose mates
have died.*

I could
be spirited into wood,
whittled
by skilled hands from red oak,
lovingly belittled
but still a feisty-looking bloke
striding across a coffee table,
or sitting with my legs crossed
on a pile of my own books,
a harmless voyeur —
Go Mary!
rising to but never
quite leaving my pursed lips —
blindly admiring salads getting tossed,
sauces enhanced, recipes glossed:
arugula, thyme, mango and leek,
and her quiescent hips.

But what a sorry
household presence I would make,
even if solid manly oak —
forever unable
to answer Mary,
engage the gamut of her looks;
or, however pungent her speech,
to hear it.
Better to speak
one last time

as her living mate
from a book, picture frame,
or evanescent chalk on a slate:
you became part of my voice,
I part of yours;
though none live twice,
to hear my voice
use yours.

Dream Wife

Though we split up some time back, she still seems
quite certain we are married — in my dreams.
Clothed — in the lobby of a nude hotel —
she corners me: *I know you all too well,*

then phones me at The Runaway Motel:
I see our marriage isn't doing very well.
Though we divorced ten years ago, it seems
legal decrees can't be enforced in dreams.

I wouldn't dream of sleeping with her now,
but here she comes claiming half my pillow.
I tell Mary, *This isn't what it seems!*
What makes us so defenseless in our dreams?

There we all live, we poor forkéd creatures,
at the mercy of our forsaken futures.

Chimera

— a beast created from parts of other beasts

A crop duster opens its wing pods,
aerosols exhale from a briefcase hissing
in an airport lounge or subway station.
EbólaPox is so ethereal
we'll have no clue a countdown has begun.
It will take us a few infinite days
to die — we will blacken, then melt away.
I'll spare you further symptoms. But terrorists

won't, nor will their feisty microallies
who gather inside us like a slow motion
nuclear bomb turning lovers and friends,
ever widening circles of strangers,
to silent singers, our bodies mouthing
hatred so primal it screams through our flesh.

Videogamer

Your cursor scurries, mouseclicks a sudden
revelation: a serial killer's face,
drawn from a neighbor's nervous description,
looks innocent of malice. Not a trace.
The life it hides you slowly scroll down,
increasingly unnervd by what you learn.
His childhood reads no different from your own!
Mom demonstrates the power of feigned concern.
A handsoff Dad confesses he's "nonplussed."
Joe seemed the kind of hustler one could trust.

Last June his college roommate disappeared.
To this day no one's found Pete or his Porsche.
Everywhere Joe goes, incredibly weird
obliterating things happen in a flash:
minds blow, fists fly, guns fire, wives die, planes crash.
Always suspected, Joe is always cleared.
Link here! You aren't depraved! You are deprived!
Your pixil double, broad in tow, shoots, flees,
confounds police with diaphanous ease —
O what a killer! And sooo multilived!

Yeah

it's about Eyerak

Let's free their terrified
off-white eyes   a whole people
congealing   in a crazed
cracked shell   feeding and warming
their yellow   sucking
yolkmeister   armed
to his smile-proof teeth   he
has them covered   from inside
out   even though   they
surround him   the whole
crush through a vast desert
moves like a mass grave
still aswarm   their deaths
a squeeze away   the meister's
oompahing heart bulging their brainpans

let's take him out   let's
cleanse   them   us   the works
let's go in   surgeons parting flesh
we squeeze   they burst   he
dazes up from a black hole
let's bury his protection
liberate his corpses   spirit
him away   into bulletproof
civilized   lawclothes   we've cut
to fit just him

Bumper Sticker Blues

THE PEOPLE harangues its masters

3 November 2004

Just call me DEMOS. Ever since Athens
partisan warfare has poisoned my veins.
I switch dysfunctions overnight: I bleed
with macho bluster, then subside toward greed,
disarming nations first *with* steel, then . . . *of* gold.
I am forever at everyone's mercy —
a groundswell of voters can make me crazy.
You decide — I only do what I'm told.

Plato believed your only sane way out
was rule by some hyper-rational wonk —
but one too decent ever to go wrong.
Now YOU'RE about to MISELECT a lout!
Has terror — *theirs* and *yours* — come on so strong?
IF YOU BELIEVE YOUR VOTE WON'T COUNT, **HONK!**

December Wedding

For Donald Junkins and Kaimei Zheng

Ye learnèd Sisters who, in times gone by
came to aid poets, help us to celebrate
the vows Kaimei and Don exchanged this morning.
Bring with you all the Nymphs that you can muster,
both of the rivers and the forests green.
On second thought, leave all those Nymphs at play.
This is a marriage of mature minds,
who, when they give their hands in love, don't blush.

My problem, Sisters, to be fairly blunt,
is English Poetry, most of whose poems
discriminate in favor of the young —
as if all couples married in their teens!
The muses are downloading their advice —
it's showing up on this computer screen.
Go tell those poems of youthful love,
they will, someday, race down the same dark street
that flows to the arena in Pamplona,

the clopping bulls, at first, no more a threat
than Time — but Time will find no better work
than test your courage every chance it gets.
Yours, Kaimei, flashes on a commune's stage
acting a part beyond the reach of Mao's plot.
Yours, Don, makes its stand on the plain white page;
sometimes the words are yours, sometimes the words
are Ernest Hemingway's, which flutter
like the muleta of an espontaneo
you wake up holding in the Plaza de Toros.

Send off:
Prince, bless the lives of Don and Kaimei, now
so firmly joined — those to whom so much has
happened: now let them happen to themselves.

The Rules of Life

For Charles Adams on his 58th, along with a copy
of Tom Watson's The Rules of Golf

14 May 1994

The Rules of Golfing are not those of Life.
The Royal and Ancient Mind anticipates
all our vicissitudes, each lurid scrape.
Is your ball plugged? You're granted a free drop —
but not nearer the hole! Drop it again.
Lost your Maxfli in Burnham Wood?
Watched it sink in the Great Bog of Cloone?
Trudge back to the tee box and strike one anew,
kissing goodbye to *stroke* and *distance* both —
in layman's speech that means you now lie three.

Once on the putting surface you may lift and clean,
but only after marking with a round flat coin.
Has your ball been seized by a crazed raccoon?
Rolled underneath mom's voluminous skirts?
Failed to fall from a palm's sticky fronds?
For such ill luck, the R & A has remedies
that speed you kindly on your golfing round.

But off the links, mere anarchy prevails.
We play by rules we mostly improvise —
or none at all — no rubrics that will bless
each misadventure with a swift, exact,
compassionate disposition.

Suppose we could persuade the wise heads
convening in the Royal and Ancient Clubhouse
to codify for us some Rules of Life?

54

We would at last know how to take relief
from hopeless situations, foreign and domestic;
know when we are entitled to improve
our lies, or toss some loose impediment aside.

What would the Royal and Ancient say
if we managed to lose our job, our wife, our mind?

Try this: "Should a wife in play go out of bounds,
or otherwise cannot be found, you may,
upon searching for her one month, no more,
put a new wife in play, assessing yourself
a penalty of half your worldly goods.

"Should a player find himself drunk with friends,
losing at politics or poker with one
more sober or more brilliant than himself,
he may declare his hand unplayable,
slip two groups sideways — but ever nearer
the bar — abandoning his hopeless cause,
losing a bit of face but no self-esteem."

The night will lie before you, failure behind.

"Upon finding yourself with nothing to say
dining with Beauty or closeted with Power —
you must blurt something every forty seconds
or else be called for delaying your own life.
Penalty: a caution the first time, then
loss of a night's pleasure or a leg up."

This does seem grim as hitting out of gorse.
I guess we cannot ask the R & A for help.
I guess we should be humbly grateful, Charles,
that one smooth green arena of our lives

has rules that are a joy to keep or break:
here's to your many mulligans and my few.

Sudden Death

On the publication of A Passion for Golf *by Laurence
Sheehan 16 October 1994 at The Edge Hill Golf Course*

Did France change Larry Sheehan? Sure it did —
though only fellow spies will know the truth —
so hear me reconstruct the swift event
that overtook him on St. Cloud's back nine
while he researched the book we celebrate.

Some have a flair for living dangerously,
but Larry's flair was always dangerous talk.
Witness his tales of counter-espionage,
witness the time he picked up on a call
to Susan while the Todds lived in a house
on subtly passionate Marlborough Street,
Susan's suave priest inviting her to "vespers"—
so claimed this man of cloth — then Larry struck:

"Why are you calling her at home — don't you know
he's here? What's that? You'll hang the usual lanterns
in Old North Church — one for her place, two for yours?
Please reconsider your vocation, Father!"

Though Susan finally reclaimed her phone
laughter imploded all her powers of speech.

No voice on earth could silence Larry Sheehan —
until he met a golfing gentleman
trudging along the back nine toward the club.
Larry had taken the wrong fork down a dogleg,
his sweating swearing foursome gang a'gley.

57

There on the 13th tee a striking man
approached him: slacks, Mephistos, black beret.
He carried but one club — a lean one-iron,
which, says Trevino, only God can hit —
see him decapitate those poppy heads!

"Would you enjoy a match with Monsieur Terme?"

"No thanks," says Larry, "time I headed back,
repaired to my Château — a deadline looms,
something Hollywood's already paid me for."

"But you've been fighting me each working day
for years . . . you know me, Larree, I'm the Prince
of Deadlines — M. Plutôt Terme." He put
a forthright hand in Larry's grasp.

                                        "Enchanté,"
says Larry, "what's your pleasure? What's our match?"

"Defeat me on these links and you'll go free.
You'll never need to face my kind again.
Surely, a fairway is a nicer place to suffer
than feeding bon mots to a hungry moniteur?"

"I know you, Buster — you black hat plagiarist! —
you're Döden from *The Seventh Seal*! Hey Mister
Death — I'm phoning Ingmar — got his number here."

"Put down your téléphone cellulaire.
You have been sweating deadlines all your life,
Larree, misery every month — wouldn't
you love to shake me off your back forever?
Go live where no one hounds you for your words?"

"What if I lose?"

"The stakes are high: you lose,
you'll nevaire fax a pizza order in on time,"

"You make an offer that has *Don't touch me,
Sucker!* tattooed all over its backside."
"Baxter would play me. So would de la Farge."*
"You got me. Hit away. Let's play for drinks."

"The only game I play is sudden death.
Our match should last one silly little hole."

So this grotesquely ill-matched pair began
the final game of golf for one of them.

Who won? Well, Larry's here. The story —
how Larry dodged the scythe-crisp one-iron
of Monsieur Plutôt Terme — can now be told.

For endless seconds, Larry froze above
a ten-foot sidehill monster for his half —
but somehow never pulled the fatal trigger.

What Larry did was saunter mildly away,
leaving his ball unputted on the 13th green.

"Not putting are you, Larree? It's your play."

"Let's just say, Fella, I was Called Away."

"No — I'm the one who must call *you* away.

---

* Baxter and de la Farge are two quasi-fictional, pathologically keen
golfers who cut a swathe through Mr. Sheehan's *A Passion for Golf.*

Your future rides on reading one putt right —
make sure your ball dies happy in the cup."

But Larry plunged on over rough and green —
Achilles striding through the asphodel,
his Maxfli whitening on the darkening green.

A small brass marker still commemorates
the spot where Larry Sheehan made his huge
refusal — il gran rifuto — at St. Cloud.

Why didn't Larry stroke that putt? If it fell,

no deadline ever would harass him more.
The only answer I can offer was a whisper
he wafted past his shoulder:

                              "Monsieur Terme,
you teach me who I am — I love you! T'aime! T'aime!
Deadlines I love, and next to deadlines, goff."

Surprising Junkins on his 65th

15 December 1996

Don, you will never sleep like the Just, or the Fulfilled.
You wake impatiently, jump-starting the laid-back dawn —
coffee and the *New York Times* consumed in the dark —
you commandeer each day against the day all days end,
yours the invisible tenseness of the amiable Samurai,
warriors sworn never to be ambushed, reaction-time
honed to meet every threat, calm every dread, seize every
        chance.
Your life is war, often without end, though the diplomat's
blitz which makes peace is always the ace up your smile.
Diplomacy and battle locked in their ancient dance
spiral dizzily together down the strands of your DNA.
You'll never sleep the sleep of fulfillment, Don,
so long as adhesive is there to be ripped from the mouths
of poets silenced by tyrants or by translators;
so long as rookie sons race back for your fungos
hit toward the gap, so long as your poem's whiplashing line
hasn't ridden its wave of feeling out to the crack of doom,
so long as the world keeps flooding your zone with zingers
it would be a crime not to pick off and score with yourself.
        Junkins,
you'll never sleep with the cool, the log-rollers, or the
        be-laureled.

Sportscast

*On the occasion of Richard Wilbur's 80th birthday,
March 2001*

Yeah, I was sassy — confrontational
even — but it would have been *criminal*
not to give Wilbur a clean open shot
at a blindsiding critic, the day
he visited C.L. Barber's poetry class.

"Sir, Randall Jarrell wrote that your poems
(I paraphrase) reminded him of something
a thoughtful tailback said about football —
how a good runner makes a choice, as each
play develops, to plunge ahead for six
or eight safe yards, or, dodging and weaving,
he goes for a possible touchdown, maybe
getting stopped cold for a big loss. Jarrell
thinks too often you, uh, settle for six."

Barber reddened, Wilbur smiled, I was thinking,
That's got to provoke a risposte mordant!
What it provoked was a mild concussion —
"I don't think Randall Jarrell wrote that review.
I believe it was Horace Gregory."

Graciousness (his) rescued embarrassment
(mine) before I could follow that folly up:
how a poet of Wilbur's caliber
should respond to a thrown gauntlet hitting
print — and whether playing it safe or going
for broke was ever a problem for him.

In the years since, I've tried to put on tape
how ABC's *Wide World of Poetry*
would broadcast highlights of Wilbur's career:

"Wilbur runs wide, the pigskin tucked away,
facing that famous Wall of Stone defense —
Lowell, Stevens, Roethke, Dickey, up front;
linebackers Nemerov, Berryman, Frost;
Hughes and Hecht at the corners, Wright and Strand
deep. No critics on this team, just brash-talking
go-for-brokers, *no way* they'll back off!

"'The *mind* is like some bat,' is the first slick
move Dick puts on the lad who think it's a hawk.
The Wall of Stone can't handle Wilbur's bat,
it's weaving rings around these groping bards!

"Now Dick shows all who've been there, done that,
'something new to see,' a Rome re-imagined!
He turns spumanti into holy water;
from various mundane ingredients
he rebuilds his own City of the Soul.
But has he trapped himself inside a *cul de sac?*"

Cameras freeze the action, spectators
wonder *en bloc*, "Can Wilbur, Stupendo
Numero Ottanta, shake himself free
from this thoroughly pagan infatuation
with that Baroque Wall Fountain drenching all
parties concerned — nymph and faun, goose and us —
in permanent, diaphanous pleasure?
Can he slip back inside the Christian fold?

"Not a problem! Dick laterals himself
across the city, over the heads of stunned

63

opponents, pleased readers — much as Deborah Kerr
lateraled herself, in *Prisoner of Zenda*,
from one Stewart Granger to another.
Within St. Peter's outstretched arms he touches
down running; two skyhigh spumes remind us
gravity brings to earth all human life,
that failure's inherent. But wait! He doesn't
abandon us before God's huge locked door;
he cuts back through the walls of Villa Sciarra
to bless those fauns, whose once distrusted bliss
ordains them now to shower reassurance:
however earthbound we believe ourselves,
our metaphors will carry us across."

Meanwhile, downstream, that ancient host of perils
looms, whose full measure he will take: he en-
tertains a godlike drunk who read minds;
God's own Mind he suddenly, perilously,
reads; a child's eyes peer out from his death bed
at something true — unconditional love! —
we never outlive. And, when the end zone's
breached, he enters, *betraying no outward
elation, as though he's been there before,*
just as Coach Vincent Lombardi advised.

About The Poet

Robert Bagg taught English at the University of Massachusetts until his retirement. His honors include a Prix de Rome, a Guggenheim Fellowship, a National Endowment for the Arts grant, a Bellagio residency, and a National Book Award nomination.

Bagg's translations of Euripides' *The Bakkhai*, *Hippolytos* and *The Cyclops* and of Sophocles' *Oedipus the King*, *Antigone* and *Women of Trakkhis* have been staged in America and abroad. He is currently at work with James Scully translating the four dramas of Sophocles not involving Oedipus.

He and his wife Mary live and work in Ashfield, Massachusetts, and are collaborating on a critical biography of Richard Wilbur.

Chimera

— a beast created from parts of other beasts

A jet opens its wing pods, aerosols
exhale from a briefcase left hissing
in an airport lounge or subway station.
EbólaPox is so ethereal
we'll have no clue a countdown has begun.
It will take us a few infinite days
to die — we will blacken, then melt away.
I'll spare you further symptoms. But terrorists

won't, nor will their feisty microallies
who gather inside us like a slow motion
nuclear bomb turning lovers and friends,
ever widening circles of strangers,
to silent singers, our bodies mouthing
hatred so primal it screams through our flesh.

Azul Editions
www.azuleditions.com

ISBN 1-885214-21-9

9 781885 214218   01200